Audience Chamber

statue

apartments for most important guests

courtyard

guests' baths

garden

small gardens

pool

rooms for less important guests

Entrance Hall

Assembly Hall

This is one of the clay tiles which were used to make the palace. The footprint was made about 2000 years ago by a child. He or she must have stepped on the tile just after it was made, when the clay was still wet.

This part of the ruined palace wall has been repaired with modern cement. You can see the shaped stones, a broken stone pillar and part of the Roman drain which stopped rainwater flooding the main courtyard.

How do we know about the Roman palace?

Finding out about the palace was like doing a giant jigsaw with most of the pieces missing. Archaeologists had to piece together different types of evidence to get a picture of life in the palace 2000 years ago.

The remains of buildings

The ruins, which were buried under the earth, had to be dug out carefully to reveal the old walls. These showed the size and shape of the palace. Pieces of plaster and mosaic showed what some of the decorations were like.

This evidence tells us that the palace was a very important building. The remains of burnt doorsteps are evidence of the fire which destroyed the palace.

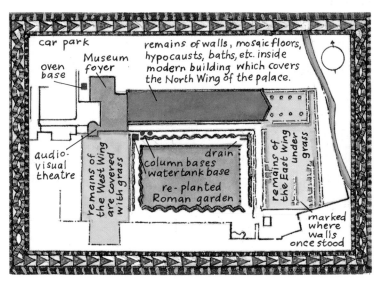

A plan of the ruins which are on show to visitors to Fishbourne today.

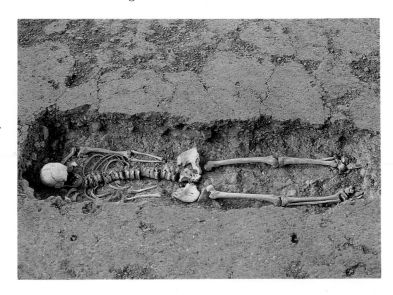

Objects from the past are often ▶ buried. They have to be excavated carefully so that no part of them is lost or broken. This skeleton was found in a grave cut through the palace floor. It is part of the evidence which tells the story of the destruction of the palace. You can find out more about this on page 7.

4

WHAT HAPPENED HERE?

ROMAN PALACE

Tim Wood

Photographs by Maggie Murray
Illustrations by Gillian Clements

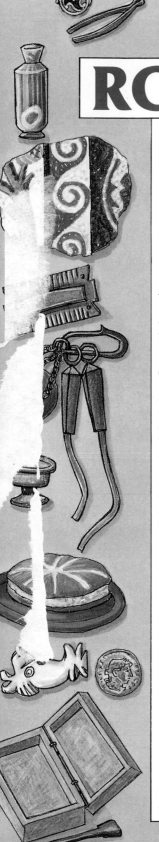

Contents

A & C BLACK · LONDON

Who lived here?

This book is about a real Roman palace. The children in this book visited the ruins of a Roman palace at Fishbourne in West Sussex. They wanted to find out what it was like to live in a Roman palace nearly 2000 years ago.

The children began their investigations in the museum which has been built over the palace ruins. They discovered that when the Romans built the palace, in about AD 75, it was the biggest and most beautiful building in Britain. Someone very important must have lived there, but no one knows who. Many historians think that the palace was the home of a British king called Tiberius Claudius Cogidubnus.

In AD 43, the Romans invaded Britain to make it part of the Roman Empire. At that time Britain was divided into tribes of people. Some British tribes fought against the Romans, but were soon beaten by the powerful Roman army.

Other British tribes welcomed the Romans. One such tribe, the Atrebates who were later called the Regni, lived in modern-day West Sussex. One of the most important men in the tribe was Tiberius Claudius Cogidubnus. We know that the Romans made him into a king under their control. Perhaps they built the palace for him as a reward for his friendship.

possible site of kitchen

main baths

Objects

In Roman times, people buried their rubbish in pits which they dug in the ground. The rubbish gives us clues about life nearly 2000 years ago. Some of the objects found at Fishbourne are shown in this book. Most are made from materials such as metal, stone, pottery, glass or bone. Can you think why this is?

Writing

Many Roman books describing life in Britain have survived. Although these books don't mention Fishbourne Palace itself, they do tell us a lot about Roman life. Letters from Roman soldiers are full of complaints about the weather in Britain. One letter is from a mother sending her son extra socks and underpants.

Can you find a piece of Roman writing in this book which is an important piece of evidence about Tiberius Claudius Cogidubnus?

Experiments can be a useful way of learning from the past. The children tried different ways of washing up Roman pots. Here they are using sand and water. They found that this method cleaned the pots quite well, but left them greasy. The Romans might have used cold wood ash which, mixed with grease, makes a kind of soap. You could try this out.

Reconstructions can tell historians a lot about life in the past. The archaeologists found trenches that the Romans dug for hedges in the palace garden. By looking at Roman books they worked out what grew in the garden. They planted Roman hedges in the trenches. Fishbourne Palace now has the only Roman garden in Britain.

Time-lines

The first time-line shows some of the important events which took place during Roman times. We do not know the exact dates of the ideas and inventions which happened between AD42 and AD450, but historians think that most of them were introduced before AD200. The second time-line shows some of the important events in the history of Fishbourne Palace, up to the present day.

Main events, ideas and inventions

AD 42

AD 42 Verica, king of the Atrebates tribe, goes to Rome to ask for help against the fierce Catuvellauni tribe. Emperor Claudius uses this as an excuse to organise a Roman invasion of Britain.

AD 43 Roman invasion of Britain. **AD 43–84** The Romans conquer most of England and Wales.

After the Roman invasion Britons have to obey Roman laws and pay Roman taxes.

Good roads with strong stone surfaces, milestones and stone bridges improve transport in Britain.

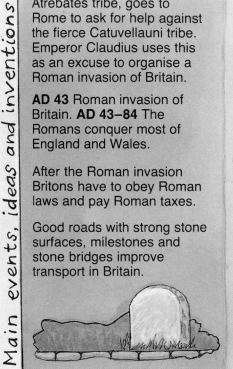

AD 60 Boudicca, queen of the Iceni tribe leads a great revolt against Roman rule in Britain. Boudicca is defeated. She takes poison and dies.

Many of the old tribal divisions in Britain start to disappear as more people behave like Romans.

Agricola, Roman governor of Britain (AD 78) defeats tribes in northern Britain and invades Scotland.

AD 87 The Romans are driven out of Scotland.

Agricola encourages the growth of tribal capitals, such as Chichester.

Properly planned towns with straight streets, large public buildings, shops and restaurants appear.

Towns get their own water supplies and sewers. Public baths and toilets introduced. Water pumps and water wheels appear.

Emperor Hadrian (AD 76–138) visits Britain in AD 122 and orders building of Hadrian's Wall.

Events at Fishbourne

AD 43

AD 43 Fishbourne becomes a supply base for the Roman army.

AD 60 A large house is built at Fishbourne.

AD 75 Fishbourne Palace built, possibly as a reward for the king of the Atrebates (Regni) tribe.

AD 100 Fishbourne Palace stops being a palace and is divided into smaller living units. New mosaics are laid.

AD 100–280 New baths built at Fishbourne Palace. New hypocaust started.

c AD 280 Part of Fishbourne Palace and everything in it destroyed by an accidental fire. No one lives in the palace again.

AD 217–270 Britain is peaceful under Roman rule.

Towns grow as more people move into them.

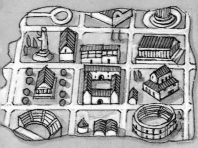

Shaped stones, mortar, concrete and plaster used for building. Tiled roofs and glass windows introduced. Mosaics and wall paintings used to decorate houses.

Many houses built with Roman central heating systems (hypocausts).

Farming improvements including better ploughs, barns, new vegetables, water mills and deeper wells introduced. More land being farmed.

Gold, silver and lead mines dug. Factories producing metal goods, pottery, glass, bricks, tiles and cloth.

Money, and official weights and measures used for trading.

Christianity becomes the official religion of the Roman Empire in AD 313.

AD 383–405 Roman Empire threatened by Civil War and Barbarian attacks. Many soldiers leave Britain to fight in Europe.

AD 408 Saxon invasion of Britain.

AD 410 Britons told by the Romans to arrange their own defences.

Various British leaders try to defend Britain against attacks by Angles, Saxons and Jutes.

AD 426–450 Roman law and order in Britain slowly breaks down. Roman towns and houses fall into disrepair.

1979

AD 300–400 Fishbourne Palace becomes a ruin. Stone and other building materials are carried off by local people to build their own houses.

AD 426–450 Fishbourne Palace forgotten, its ruins gradually covered over with dirt.

1938 Children living in a house close to the site of Fishbourne Palace discover a black and white Roman mosaic in their back garden.

1960 Workers digging a trench for a water pipe find the ruins of Fishbourne Palace.

1960–68 The site of the Palace excavated. Over 1,000 people volunteer to help. A large building put over this site and opened as Fishbourne Roman Palace and Museum.

1979 Conservation work begins. Mosaics lifted and transferred onto waterproof, concrete bases.

How the palace was built

The children discovered that Fishbourne Palace was built just 32 years after the Romans invaded Britain. At that time most people in Britain lived in wooden huts. The Britons wouldn't have had the knowledge or skill to build this huge stone palace. It must have been built by the Romans – almost certainly by workers brought from other parts of the Roman Empire.

Roman surveyors probably measured the site and marked where the walls had to go. Other skilled craftworkers cut, shaped and laid stones.

It seems likely that the Romans used British workers to help them. The Romans probably trained some Britons to shape stone, cut wood and build walls. Other Britons were slaves who dug holes and carried heavy loads.

Roman windows were small, perhaps to keep burglars out. This reconstructed Roman window at Fishbourne Palace has modern glass in it. Roman glass was cloudier and hard to see through.

The children used some real Roman tiles to discover how the palace roof was made. They found that each flat tile, called a tegula, slotted into the next. A curved tile, called an imbrex, covered the gap between two tegulae to stop the rain getting in.

This part of the palace wall is still standing. Two broken columns in this wall were an important clue about the rest of the palace. By measuring the distance between the columns, archaeologists worked out how many columns there were around the main courtyard.

Cargo ships carried building materials such as stones for the palace walls from all over the Roman Empire to Chichester harbour. The harbour was close to the site of the palace. Soldiers cut the stones with iron bars and chisels, and smoothed them with sand. By examining the ruins, the children found how the builders made the walls from a double row of shaped limestone blocks cemented together with limestone mortar. The builders filled the hollow space between the two rows of blocks with rubble.

Inside the palace

Most of the palace is now in ruins but archaeologists have pieced together tiny fragments of plaster to discover that Fishbourne Palace used to be very grand inside. The walls were plastered with lime to make them smooth, then they were painted. Some walls were painted to look like marble. Others had whole scenes on them. One wall had a painting of a garden, while another showed a bowl of fruit. The ceilings were made from bundles of reeds, which were also plastered. Some ceilings had shapes moulded into the plaster. Others had patterns painted on them.

Part of a beautiful mosaic floor at Fishbourne Palace. The children investigated how mosaics were made. They learned that mosaic makers made the main outline of the pattern by pressing the best, squarest tesserae into wet mortar. They filled in the rest of the pattern using smaller and less regular tiles.

Mosaics were pictures or patterns made with small stone tiles called tesserae. The Romans made mosaics which covered the floors of many rooms.

At the time when Fishbourne Palace was built, the Britons did not know how to make mosaics or wall paintings. The children compared the first mosaics made at Fishbourne with the later ones.

They found that the early mosaics were very complicated and must have been made by skilled workers who came from another part of the Roman Empire. Some of the later mosaics were not so well made. They were probably made by British workers who had been taught some of the skills of mosaic making.

This girl tried sawing stone using a smooth iron blade and sand. She found it very hard going, but it did work. The Romans used a method like this to cut and smooth blocks of building stone. They also made long thin rods of stone which they cut into square tesserae.

This girl made a mosaic in a sand tray using real Roman tesserae. The king decided which patterns would cover the palace floors. He probably chose the shapes and pictures from a book of patterns shown to him by the mosaic makers.

11

Work

There is no written evidence about what went on in the palace. But from the size of the building and the number of rooms we know that it must have been a very busy place. About 250 people probably lived there. This number included the king and his family, servants, slaves, guards, office workers called scribes, and craftworkers, as well as important Roman and British visitors.

Tiberius Claudius Cogidubnus must have worked hard, ruling his kingdom and meeting for talks with other British leaders. He had to make his people pay taxes to Rome and obey Roman laws. Scribes collected the taxes which had to be sent regularly to Rome. They kept the king's accounts and records up to date. Some of the glass counters and rounded pebbles they used to do sums have been found at Fishbourne.

The children filled a Roman-style pottery lamp with olive oil. When the children lit the lamp, they found it gave a very dim light. They guessed from this that Tiberius Claudius Cogidubnus did not stay up late at night working. He probably went to bed early in the evening and got up at dawn so he could work in daylight.

The children tried the beeswax tablets used by Roman scribes. They scratched words in the wax with wood or metal styluses. Some Roman records were written in ink on scrolls. The scrolls were made of papyrus, an early type of paper. Several inkwells have been found in the palace ruins.

Slaves worked all day long cleaning the hundred rooms in the palace, preparing meals and looking after the king, his family and their visitors. This boy swept the kitchen which has been reconstructed at Fishbourne, using sand to polish the floor as Roman slaves did.

The children discovered that the palace had a huge Audience Chamber where visitors, some of them from Rome, would have met with Tiberius Claudius Cogidubnus. The children found some of the guest rooms where the visitors stayed.

Keeping warm

We know from Roman books about Britain that the Romans, who came from Italy, found the British weather damp and cold. In winter, the Romans warmed their houses with bronze heaters, called braziers, which held wood or charcoal. Slaves carried the braziers around to warm different rooms.

Many large Roman houses had an underfloor central heating system, called a hypocaust. The hypocaust worked very well, although there was no real way of controlling the heat. We know that some Romans had to wear wooden clogs indoors to protect their feet from floors which were too hot!

Part of the unfinished hypocaust at Fishbourne Palace. These brick pillars were built to hold up a floor. Hot air from a furnace would have circulated between the pillars under the floor and passed up through hollow box-shaped tiles in the walls.

furnace

floo

Fishbourne Palace has a fine hypocaust, but it may never have been used because the palace burnt down before it was finished. It seems likely that braziers warmed the palace for most of the time. The children thought that some of the larger rooms must have been very cold in winter. Perhaps one day a Roman Briton knocked over a brazier and that's what started the fire which burned the palace down.

The children looked at some Roman box tiles used in a hypocaust. The tiles fitted together to make chimneys inside the walls. The children found the outsides of the tiles were rough. This helped the plaster stick to them. Inside the tiles the children found some Roman soot.

This diagram shows how the hypocaust worked. Slaves kept the furnace going with wood.

hot air

The builders might have laid a mosaic floor something like this over the floor of the hypocaust in the palace.

Keeping clean

The Romans built public baths wherever they went. They loved bathing and thought that being clean was very important. The Roman Britons copied this habit.

Fishbourne Palace had three sets of baths. The main baths, at the south-east corner (look back at the drawing of the palace on page 2), were very large. There was a hot room, called a caldarium, where bathers could swim in a hot pool. Bathers could also swim in the pool in a cold room called a frigidarium.

These two clay pipes could be joined tightly. They probably carried water. Pipes similar to these carried water to the fountains in the garden at Fishbourne Palace.

In a warm room, called a tepidarium, bathers had a massage, or cleaned themselves by rubbing olive oil on their bodies. They scraped off the oil and dirt with a curved scraper called a strigil, several of which have been found in the ruins of other Roman baths.

oil jar

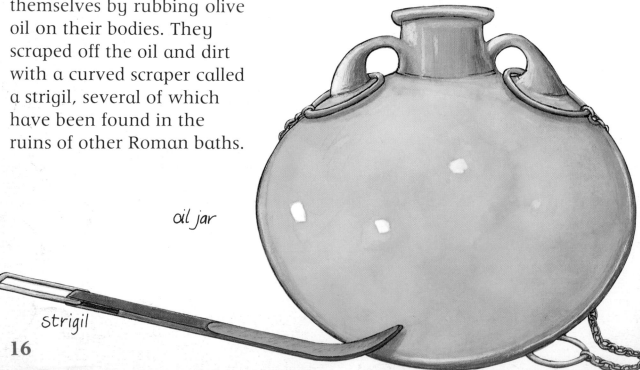

strigil

One of the other sets of baths, in the north wing, was smaller. They were next to the guest rooms, so the children guessed that visitors to the palace used them. In the main courtyard the children found the remains of a huge stone water tank which stored the water for the fountains in the garden. But they could find no signs of a tank for the bath water or the furnaces which the slaves stoked with wood to heat the water.

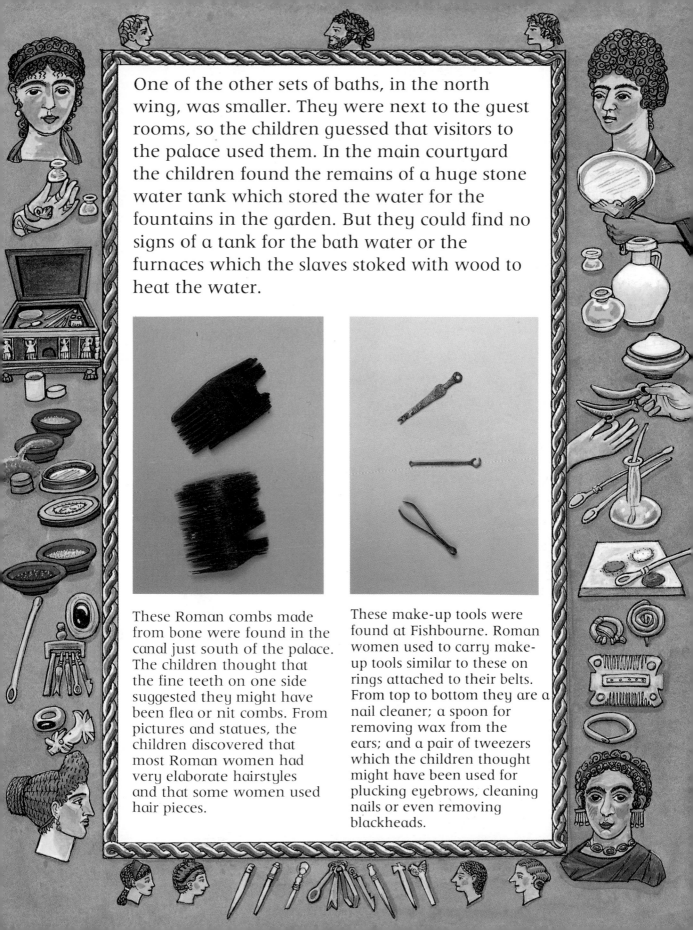

These Roman combs made from bone were found in the canal just south of the palace. The children thought that the fine teeth on one side suggested they might have been flea or nit combs. From pictures and statues, the children discovered that most Roman women had very elaborate hairstyles and that some women used hair pieces.

These make-up tools were found at Fishbourne. Roman women used to carry make-up tools similar to these on rings attached to their belts. From top to bottom they are a nail cleaner; a spoon for removing wax from the ears; and a pair of tweezers which the children thought might have been used for plucking eyebrows, cleaning nails or even removing blackheads.

Getting dressed

We know from written evidence that some Britons copied Roman fashions. Almost everyone who lived in the palace must have worn Roman tunics. Rich people had tunics made of fine wool, linen or even silk. Poor people wore tunics made of rough wool. Some very important men wore togas over their tunics. Some togas were plain, others had coloured borders to show that the wearers were important people. Togas and tunics came in many different colours. The Roman Britons used plants to dye cloth, such as woad for blue tints and madder for red.

◀ The children tried putting on a toga. The toga is just like a woollen blanket up to six metres long. One end was draped over the wearer's shoulder, while the other end was tucked into the wearer's belt.

The three children in the front of this group are dressed like slaves, in simple tunics. The girl behind is wearing a stola. The boy wearing the toga has a bulla round his neck. This is a leather bag containing a charm, often shaped like a wheel, which the Romans wore for good luck. ▶

Rich women wore brightly coloured woollen, cotton or even silk dresses, called stolas, over their tunics. On top they wore long shawls called pallas. Pallas could be draped in many ways. Women often wrapped them over their heads when they went out.

Many people wore leather sandals. These came in various different shapes and sizes. Women wore colourful, light sandals. Soldiers wore heavy sandals called caligae which were made of thick stiff leather with hobnails in the soles. We know from statues that the Romans sometimes wore socks, especially in countries which were colder than Italy.

This boy tried on a Roman sandal.

19

What did the Romans eat?

The palace had a large kitchen garden. Using evidence from gardens at other Roman sites, archaeologists worked out that much of the fruit, vegetables and herbs eaten by the king were probably grown in the garden of Fishbourne Palace. The Romans brought many new vegetables with them when they came to Britain, including lettuce, cabbage and cauliflower.

Part of the Roman kitchen garden at Fishbourne now contains plants which the Romans ate. This boy picked some rosemary, one of the herbs which the Romans used to flavour their food.

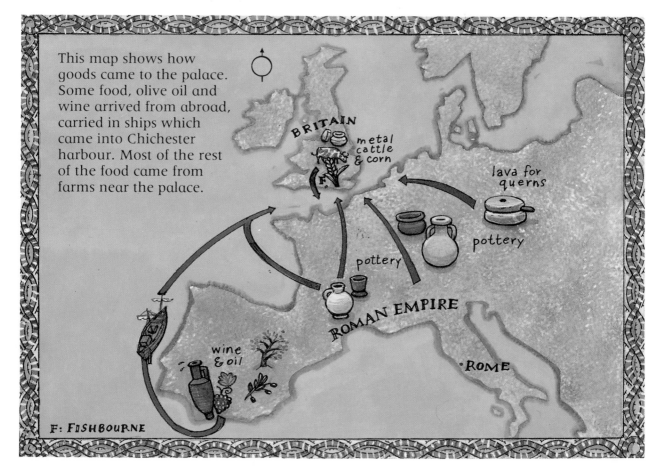

This map shows how goods came to the palace. Some food, olive oil and wine arrived from abroad, carried in ships which came into Chichester harbour. Most of the rest of the food came from farms near the palace.

BRITAIN

metal cattle & corn

lava for querns

pottery

pottery

ROMAN EMPIRE

ROME

wine & oil

F: FISHBOURNE

Looking at a map, the children found that the Roman town of Chichester was just a few kilometres away from the palace. They thought that slaves may have bought some of the food for the palace at the shops and markets there.

Keeping food fresh was a big problem in Roman times because there were no cans or fridges. A lot of the food eaten by the king, his family and his visitors must have been delivered every day to the door of the palace from nearby farms. Some of the food might have been brought in carts so the cooks could choose what they wanted. Some farmers must have delivered live animals to be killed at the palace whenever meat was needed.

In Roman times olive oil, fish sauce and wine were carried and stored in large pots called amphorae. The children found that three of them could only just lift a Roman-style amphora when it was full. After pouring away most of the water, this boy was able to lift the amphora. The stubby handle at the pointed end made the amphora easier to use.

When the palace was first built, the sea was very close by. Many shells, net weights, fish hooks and large needles for making and mending nets have been found in the ruins of the palace. Fishing boats may have tied up at a dock near the palace every day to sell fish and shellfish to the palace cooks.

Preparing food

Kitchen slaves prepared all the food for the king, his staff and visitors to the palace. We don't know where the kitchen was at Fishbourne Palace but it must have been similar to the Roman kitchens which archaeologists have found in other places.

In Pompeii in Italy complete houses have been found perfectly preserved by the ash from a volcano which destroyed the town in AD 79 – even down to the meals which were left on the tables.

This boy pounded spices in a pottery pestle and mortar just as a Roman slave would have done.

We know from this evidence that the kitchen slaves washed vegetables in stone sinks and chopped them on wooden tables using sharp iron knives. They ground grains such as wheat or barley into flour using hand mills called querns.

The Roman Britons used many cooking tools similar to those which you may have in your kitchen, including graters, ladles and baking trays. Some of these tools, as well as knives, pots and other cooking items were stored on shelves or hung on hooks around the kitchen walls.

The children tried using a quern in the reconstructed Roman kitchen at Fishbourne Palace. One of them dropped grain through a hole in the top of the quern. The other turned the handle to make the top stone rub against the bottom stone. The flour trickled out through the gap between the stones.

One of the children used a Roman-style pottery sieve to get rid of the grain which had not been ground properly by the quern. The Romans used sieves like this to drain cheese, and to sieve wine and sauces.

Cooking

The Roman kitchen stove was a raised stone hearth which looked something like a modern barbecue. The open top of the hearth was filled with charcoal. The burning charcoal must have made the kitchen very hot for the slaves who worked there.

Most Roman cooking pots were made of pottery, although some were iron. The pots stood on iron stands to keep them out of the red-hot charcoal.

The children tried cooking some Roman meals on a reconstructed cooking platform in the garden at Fishbourne Palace. This girl baked a fish with herbs. She had to keep turning the fish so that it wouldn't burn.

These pots were found in a Roman rubbish pit at Fishbourne. The pots were broken and have all been repaired.

24

The children made the thick vegetable stew called pulmentus which the palace slaves ate at most meals. The pulmentus looked disgusting, but the children found that it was quite pleasant to eat. You can find the recipe for pulmentus on page 30.

Food could be boiled or fried in a pottery pan on the open hearth, boiled in a big pot over an open fire, roasted on a spit, or baked in an oven. The remains of an oven have been found in Fishbourne Palace, so we know that the slaves at Fishbourne baked for the king and his court. But most ordinary houses and flats in Roman towns had no oven, so the people who lived in them had to buy their bread, cakes and puddings from a baker.

A feast

The Romans and Roman Britons ate small breakfasts and lunches. They liked bread or wheat biscuits with honey, dates or olives. They ate their main meal in the late afternoon. Poor people ate porridge and vegetables. Rich people feasted. The children decided that Tiberius Claudius Cogidubnus must often have had magnificent banquets to entertain friends and important visitors.

Food for a Roman feast. Most of the food was served on fine red pottery, called samian ware, although Tiberius Claudius Cogidubnus may have had silver or even gold dishes. The children tried all the food and were surprised how delicious it tasted. They were shocked to hear that Romans thought it was very polite to belch at table!

A three-course feast

GUSTATIO
~starters~
salads
olives
shellfish
snails fattened with milk
eggs or dormice
sprinkled with honey
& poppyseeds
ALL SERVED WITH
LIQUAMEN!
(a strong fish sauce)

PRIMA MENSA
~First course~

roast boar
roast duck with damsons
roast suckling pig
boiled lamb

SECUNDA MENSA
~Second course~

cheese
spiced loaves
honey cakes
fruit
stuffed dates

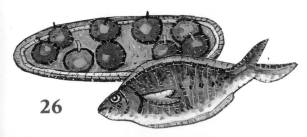

Banquets were served in the dining room. Only the floor of this room is left at Fishbourne, but there are many descriptions of feasts in Roman books and letters. We know from these that guests lay on couches and ate with their fingers, or with spoons.

Slaves brought in the food and carved the meat. They took towels round so the guests could wipe their fingers between courses. To entertain the diners, the slaves played musical instruments such as pipes, lyres, flutes and tambourines. On special occasions performances were given by dancers, acrobats, jugglers and conjurers and the works of famous poets were sometimes read aloud.

The reconstructed dining room at Fishbourne Palace contains Roman-style furniture.

These broken pieces of Roman glass were found in the ruins of the palace. The glass jug and bowl are modern, but they have been made in Roman shapes. Glass was often used at feasts because it did not spoil the taste of the food or drink. The Romans drank watered wine or mulsum (wine sweetened with honey) with their meals.

Giving thanks to the gods

The Romans had many gods and goddesses. They went to temples to pray to their most important gods, to make sacrifices or to take part in grand festivals. The children discovered that Tiberius Claudius Cogidubnus had ordered a temple to Neptune and Minerva to be built not far from the palace. Perhaps he went there sometimes to thank the gods.

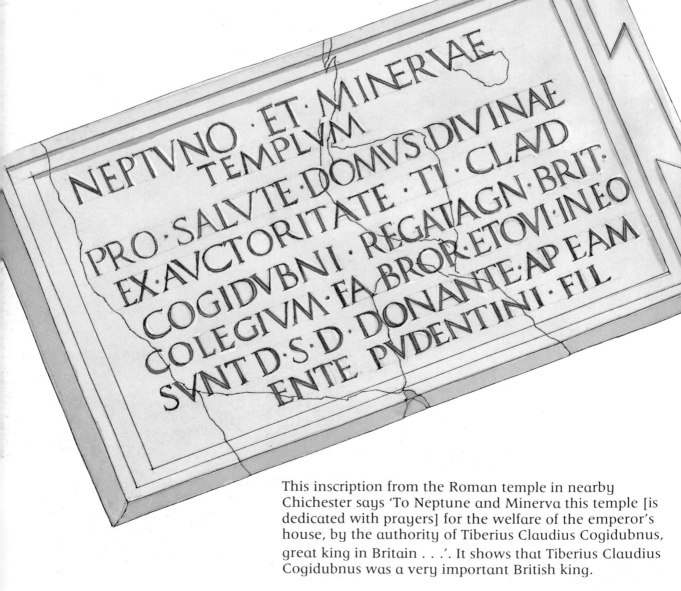

NEPTVNO · ET · MINERVAE
TEMPLVM
PRO · SALVTE · DOMVS DIVINAE
EX · AVCTORITATE · TI · CLAVD
COGIDVBNI · REGATAGN · BRIT·
COLEGIVM · FA BROR · ETOVI · INEO
SVNT D · S · D · DONANTE · AP · EAM
ENTE PVDENTINI · FIL

This inscription from the Roman temple in nearby Chichester says 'To Neptune and Minerva this temple [is dedicated with prayers] for the welfare of the emperor's house, by the authority of Tiberius Claudius Cogidubnus, great king in Britain . . .'. It shows that Tiberius Claudius Cogidubnus was a very important British king.

The Romans believed their homes were watched over by household spirits called numina. Some numina had names, such as Vesta, goddess of the hearth, and Janus, god of doorways.

Other spirits, called lares, looked after the people in the house. The Romans built shrines for these household spirits in their homes. They prayed to them each day and gave them little gifts of food and wine.

An original limestone dea nutrix found near Fishbourne. She may once have held a baby in her arms.

The lares, or little mother goddess, which was thought to bring fruitfulness was kept in a small shrine called a lararium. Some lares held baskets of food. Others, like the model shown here called a dea nutrix, were shown nursing babies. One of the children sprinkled salt over the dea nutrix at Fishbourne, as the Romans did, for good luck.

How to find out more

Visits

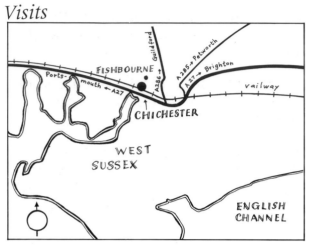

You can visit Fishbourne Roman Palace, Salthill Road, Fishbourne, Chichester, West Sussex PO19 3QR. Tel: 01243 785859. School parties or groups can do most of the activities shown in this book by arrangement with the Education Officer.

There are many other excellent places you can visit to learn more about life in Roman times. Among the best are Verulamium Museum, St Michael's, St Albans, Herts AL3 4SW, tel: 01727 751810; The Museum of London, 150 London Wall, London EC2Y 5HN, tel: 020 7600 3699; The Corinium Museum, Park Street, Cirencester, Gloucestershire GL7 2BX, tel: 01285 655611; The Roman Baths Museum, Pump Rooms, Stall Street, Bath BA1 1LZ, tel: 01225 477784.

For information on suitable places to visit in your area, contact:
English Heritage Education Service
Tel: 020 7973 3442/3
Historic Scotland
Tel: 0131 668 8600
The National Trust
Tel: 020 7222 9251

Things to do

Here are some ideas for things to do which will help you to find out more about life in Roman times.

Try out some Roman recipes
You will need an adult to help you.

Carrots in peppered wine sauce
Thinly slice 8 medium carrots lengthwise, and sauté them in ½ cup white wine, ½ cup vegetable stock, 2 teaspoons of olive oil and 1 teaspoon of pepper until done.

Serve the carrots with the sauce.

Fish cooked in its own juice
Clean, wash and dry a salmon, salmon trout or trout. Pound 1 tablespoon (15ml) each of salt and coriander in a mortar. Roll the fish in this mixture.

Put the fish in an ovenproof frying pan, seal by frying quickly on both sides then cover with a lid.

Put the pan in the oven and bake at gas mark 4 (350°F, 180°C) until the fish is cooked through.

Remove from oven, sprinkle the fish with 1 tablespoon (15ml) of strong vinegar then serve.

Pulmentus
Take a mixture of soaked wheat grains and pulses such as peas, beans or lentils.

Boil them together for an hour or until they are soft. The mixture should look something like lumpy porridge!

Dye some cloth the Roman way

You will need an adult to help you.

Wearing rubber gloves, soak some clean wool or material in rainwater. While this is soaking, fill an aluminium saucepan with onion skins and add soft water (rainwater is best) to within 5cm of the top of the pan.

Simmer the mixture gently for 15–20 minutes, then allow it to cool. Strain the liquid and pour it back into the pan. Put the wool or material into the pan.

Bring to the boil and simmer for 30 minutes. Turn off the heat and allow the dye to cool.

When the liquid is cold, lift out the wool or material. Rinse and allow to dry naturally. What colour is it?

You can use exactly the same method with walnut husks except you must first soak 250gm of husks overnight in 2 litres of water and a tablespoon of vinegar.

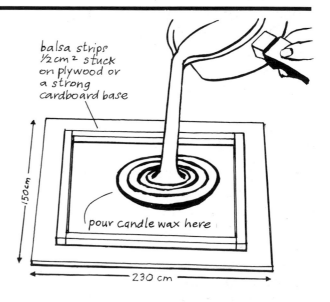

Make a Roman writing tablet

You will need an adult to help you.

Make the base of the tablet by sticking strips of balsa wood ½cm² round the edge of a piece of plywood or strong cardboard about 150cm wide by 230cm long.

Put candle stubs in an old saucepan and heat gently to allow the wax to melt. Pour the melted wax into the base.

Ask an adult to carve the stylus from a piece of balsa wood. One end should be pointed for writing and the other end should be flat for rubbing out.

balsa strips ½cm² stuck on plywood or a strong cardboard base

150cm

pour candle wax here

230 cm

Index

First paperback edition 2000

First published 1994 in hardback by
A & C Black (Publishers) Limited
35 Bedford Row
London WC1R 4JH

ISBN 0-7136-5366-3

© 1994 A & C Black (Publishers) Limited

A CIP catalogue record for this book is available from the British Library.

Books in the series available in hardback:
Roman Fort
Tudor Farmhouse
Tudor Warship
Victorian Factory

Acknowledgements
The author and publishers would like to thank the Sussex Archaeological Society; the owners and administrators of Fishbourne Roman Palace and their staff, especially David Rudkin (Director), Wendy Austin-Ward (Education Officer), Claire Ryley (Assistant Education Officer); Catherine and Edward Davenport; Georgina and Edward Taylor; Lucy Webb; Cressida Rudkin; Emma Austin-Ward; Jenny Punter; Josh and Miranda Punter; Marilyn Tolhurst; Monica Stoppleman; and Elizabeth Newbery.

The photograph on page 29 (left) appears by kind permission of Mr D.C. Bland.

Typeset in Meridien 14/17pt
by Rowland Phototypesetting Limited
Bury St Edmunds, Suffolk.

Printed and bound in Italy by L.E.G.O.